A9

D0879467

ROMANTIK

Preface

It's obvious that we are constantly trying to expand the possibilities of modern computer graphics. Still, vector graphics can sometimes look rather sterile and recent attempts have been made to make them warmer and more human. That's why, for example, in the last two to three years graphics or photos are often accented with handwritten scribbles or text that purposely offset and break up their sleekness and brilliance. In this way, the artwork becomes more personal and is often used in situations where a feeling of closeness or commitment should be generated.

"Romantik" presents an additional approach to expanding the forms of visual expression available in our computer-dominated world. The title "Romantik" is more than a modern reference to its classical definition from the 19th century – the heyday of salon art, when paintings were the TVs of their time and leisure traveling a privilege of the rich. German Romanticism (1794 – 1835) as well as English literature and poetry were a rehearsal of the rebellion against (French) Enlightenment. Mary Shelley (1797 – 1851) wrote the novel "Frankenstein", subtitled "The Modern Prometheus", in 1818. This novel describes a being, which is chained to a machine instead of a cliff. The Romanticists not only practiced rebellion against but also criticized the Age of Enlightenment for its technology, trust in the future and society of the masses as well as its pursuit of clarity, rationalism and abjuration.

Classical Romanticism opposed the Enlightenment with abstraction, passion, longing, nature, the past, the individual as redeemer and the transience of being. These components were symbolized via analogies and symbols such as candles, hearts, sunsets, flowers, animals, ornaments and tendrils as well as through Jesus, saints and religious relics. Today's definition of "kitsch" as an overly ornate and copiously emotional aesthetic form of expression arose from the Romantic period. And the boundary between "Romantik" and kitsch is still as blurred as ever.

Today, many "Romantik" approaches and motifs can be found in modern design and art. These include not only references to the hippie era, the rock music record covers of the 60s and 70s and Art Nouveau, but also the "New Romantic" movement of the 80s with its exotic clothing, dandy-ish behavior and penchant for arches, crests and Tudor motifs. All of these styles are in again. Indeed almost everything that precedes desktop publishing (DTP) is enjoying renewed popularity.

It appears that today's designers are being influenced by all of the Romantic eras before DTP simultaneously without any ideological qualification. The "New Romantic" (chic) and hippie (sloppy) cultures are, for example, more opposite than similar. They offer almost no contextual intersection other than the fact that they both have contributed to the Romanticism of the early 21rst century. Indeed the main goal of modern "Romantik" was to stand in contrast to the typical style of the end of the last century through all available means. Instead of uncluttered surfaces, there were collages. Instead of clean lines, ornament was used to define a room.

The fact that "Romantik" has a different view of the self and especially of transcendence is particularly important. The 90s were positivistic, demonstrable and realistic if not hyper-realistic. Solutions and possibilities lay within the self; feelings were adjusted to the needs of the moment through "emotional engineering" that was helped along by drugs such as Prozac and Ecstasy. The search for transcendence was self-determined and took place in the molecular and chemical arena. There was no God and no fate. If anything, there were bad drugs. Today, on the other hand, one is less self-determined and is more likely to believe in inevitable external forces. Transcendence is again manifesting itself as longing and abstraction and in poses that are becoming ever more similar. The subject doesn't look toward the viewer but heavenward into the unending distance where dreams that are not realizable on earth can be projected. This corresponds to the "Romantik" view with its fateful errors and tumult as well as the longing for positions that can be resolved in a non-rational way.

Today's "Romantik" approach is pragmatic rather than dogmatic. The computer is established as a creative tool and almost no one can think of working without one anymore. Still, it appears as though the use of the computer's traditional strengths, such as those found in vector graphics, is no longer considered a virtue or an end in itself. Instead, the role of the computer in the design process is being challenged. We'd much rather see the computer as a tool and as a mechanical servant of humanity than as our idol. And this is a view that is sure to please the romantics of all eras.

Robert Klanten

VORWORT

Es ist offensichtlich, dass moderne Computergraphik ständig versucht, ihr Material, ihre Möglichkeiten zu erweitern. Dabei wird in letzter Zeit versucht, die manchmal als steril empfundene Vektorgraphik zu vermenschlichen, ihr einen wärmeren Anstrich zu geben. Deshalb werden z.B. Graphik oder Photo mit handgemachten „Kritzeleien" oder Textpassagen versehen, ihre Glätte und Brillanz damit gezielt aufgehoben und gebrochen. Die Arbeiten werden persönlicher und oftmals dort eingesetzt, wo Anwendungen Nähe und Verbindlichkeit erzeugen sollen.

„Romantik" präsentiert einen weiteren Ansatz, die Ausdrucksformen zu erweitern.

Das Buch „Romantik" hat einen klaren Bezug zur klassischen Definition des Begriffes aus dem 19. Jahrhundert. Es war die Periode der Salonkunst, in der Gemälde die Fernseher ihrer Zeit waren und das Reisen aus Vergnügen den Reichen vorbehalten war. Die Deutsche Romantik (1794 – 1835) und englische Literatur und Lyrik probten den Aufstand gegen das Zeitalter der (französischen) Aufklärung. Von Mary Shelley (1797 – 1851) stammt der Roman „Frankenstein" (1818), dessen Untertitel lautet „Der Moderne Prometheus", und beschreibt ein Wesen, dass an die Maschine statt an einen Felsen gekettet ist. Die Romantik übte Kritik an und probte den Aufstand gegen die Aufklärung und deren Streben nach Klarheit, Verstand, Entsagung, Technologie und Maschinen, Zukunftsglauben, die Gesellschaft der Massen.

Die Klassische Romantik setzte dem entgegen: Zwielicht, Gefühl und Leidenschaft, Verlangen, Natur, die Vergangenheit, das Individuum als Erlöser, die Vergänglichkeit des Seins und fand ihre Analogien und Zeichen in Kerzen und Herzen, Sonnenuntergängen, Pflanzen, Tieren, Natur allgemein, Ornamenten, Ranken aber auch in Jesus, Heiligen, Devotionalien. Aus der Romantik entstand die heutige Definition des Kitsch als überladene und weitschweifige, emotionalisierte, ästhetische Ausdrucksform und somit sind die Übergänge zwischen Romantik und Kitsch stets noch fliessend.

Heute lassen sich viele romantischen Ansätze und Motive in modernen Anwendungen nachweisen, Referenzen an die Hippieära, Rockmusik-Plattencover der 60er und 70er Jahre und Jugendstil, aber auch an die „New Romantic" der 80er Jahre mit ihren exotischen Verkleidungen, dandyhaftem Benehmen, der Vorliebe für Bombierungen, Wappen und Tudormotive, all dies findet wieder Anklang. Hauptsache prä-dtp.

Es scheint, als ob heutige Designer sich von allen „romantischen" Perioden vor DTP gleichzeitig beeinflussen lassen, ohne ideologische Ausschlusskriterien zu befolgen, denn „New Romantic" (schick) und Hippiekultur (schlampig) stehen sich eher gegenüber denn nahe und bieten kaum inhaltliche Überschneidungen. Sie bedienen aber beide gleichzeitig die „Romantik" des frühen 21. Jahrhunderts. Hauptsache erscheint die Abgrenzung gegenüber den Stilmitteln der 90er, denn wo aufgeräumte Flächen waren, finden sich jetzt Collagen, wo klare Linien den Raum definierten, stehen jetzt Ornamente.

Wichtig dabei erscheint das unterschiedliche Selbstverständnis, ja besonders die Frage der Transzendenz.
Die Neunziger waren positivistisch, selbstbestimmt beweisbar, realistisch bis hyperrealistisch. Die Lösungen und Möglichkeiten lagen in einem selbst, Gefühle wurden mittels „emotional engineering" den Bedürfnissen angepasst. Dabei halfen Drogen wie Prozac und Ecstasy. Die Suche nach Transzendenz wurde im molekularen, im chemischen Bereich betrieben und war selbstbstimmt. Es gab keinen Gott und kein Schicksal, allenfalls schlechte Drogen.
Heutzutage ist man weniger selbstbestimmt, glaubt eher an unabwendbare, äussere Einflüsse.
Transzendenz manifestiert sich wieder in abstraktem Verlangen und Entrücktheit, in immer ähnlichen Posen. So schaut der Abgebildete oftmals nicht zum Betrachter, sondern himmelwärts in die endlose Ferne, dorthin, wo irdisch nicht realisierbare Träume projiziert werden. Dies entspricht den Auffassungen der Romantik, mit ihren schicksalhaften Irrungen und Wirrungen und dem Verlangen nach nicht rational auflösbaren Positionen.

Die heutige Herangehensweise an die Arbeiten ist aber pragmatisch und nicht dogmatisch geprägt, niemand käme auf die Idee keinen Computer mehr als Werkzeug zu benutzen. Es scheint nur so, dass die Abbildung und Überhöhung der klassischen Stärken des Computers, wie Vektorgraphik, nicht mehr als Selbstzweck oder Tugend begriffen, sondern auf ihren Nutzen im Gestaltungsprozess hinterfragt werden. Dem Computer wird dabei lieber ein Werkzeugcharakter zuwiesen, die Maschine als Knecht des Menschen und nicht als sein Idealbild aufgefasst. Eine Sichtweise, die den Romantikern aller Zeiten durchaus gefallen dürfte.

Robert Klanten

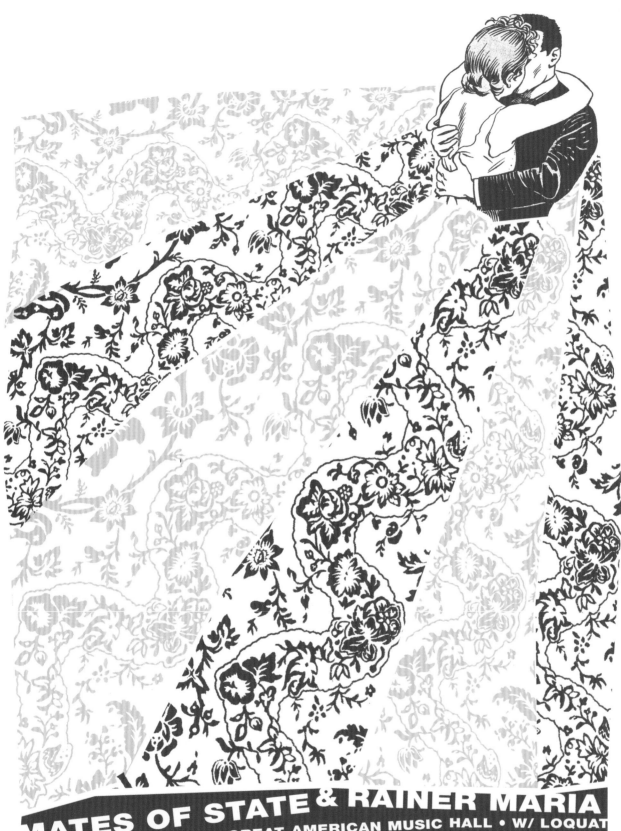

MATES OF STATE & RAINER MARIA

FEBRUARY 20 • GREAT AMERICAN MUSIC HALL • W/ LOQUAT

FEBRUARY 21 • BOTTOM OF THE HILL • W/ DEAR NORA

TWO SHOWS
ALL AGES

PEDRO THE LION

MAY 21 • GREAT AMERICAN MUSIC HALL
W/ THE STRATFORD 4 • STARFLYER 59 • ESTER DRANG

~ Jason Munn

hjärn

bang om biologism

ISABEL MARANT

ISABEL MARANT

side A 1. Let's Step Aside 2. Frosted Minds 3. It's Golden 4. I'm Not myself 5. Open Those Eyes 6. Say oh Say
side B 1. Three-minute Convert 2. Don't Remind Me 3. Naked Natives 4. She's so Ready 5. Preacher/Songwriter 6. Tigersuite

Recorded at Studio Gröndahl, Stockholm and Åträsk bygdegård, Åträsk. Additional recordings at Second Home, Umeå, Rumble Road Studio, Skellefteå and Musikstenen, Umeå.
a1, a2, b1, b2 and b4 recorded and produced by Pelle Gunnerfeldt and Isolation Years. a5 and b3 recorded and produced by Johan Gustafsson and Isolation Years.
a3, a4, a6, b5 and b6 recorded and produced by Isolation Years. Mixed by Pelle Gunnerfeldt at Studio Gröndahl, except b5, mixed by Johannes Berglund.
Mastered by Sören Eronsson at Cosmos Mastering, Stockholm. String arrangement on b1 by Björn Yttling. All instruments played by Isolation Years except: Oscar Brändström
saxophone on a2 and b6 Daniel Johansson, trumpet on a2 and b3 flugelhorn on b3, Andreas Forsman violins on b1. Lovisa Nyström vocals on b1 and background vocals on a3.
All songs published by MNW Music AB/Picnic Music Publishing. Administration by Warner/Chappell Music Scandinavia AB.
Management: Hansi Friberg/Black Star Management. www.blackstarmanagement.com Thanks: Henrik, Johannes, Hansi, Robin.
Jeannette, Rolf, Per H, Oscar, Daniel J. Lovisa N, Pelle G, Johan G, Nåra och Kårel. Design by io. www.isolationyears.com

plej

ELECTRONIC MUSIC FROM THE SWEDISH LEFTCOAST

A
Au Naturel

B
From Here To Where?
And Still They Point At You

THENEWMESS
Au Naturel

dLTD

dLTD 005 © & ℗ Deleted Art 2003
Deleted Art, c/o Samsonowitz, Lars Kaggsgatan 43 a, S-415 04 Gothenburg, Sweden
www.deletedart.org, info@deletedart.org

NITRADA 0+

1

2

1. Robert Samsonowitz - 2. Nihada ❧ ❦ 12

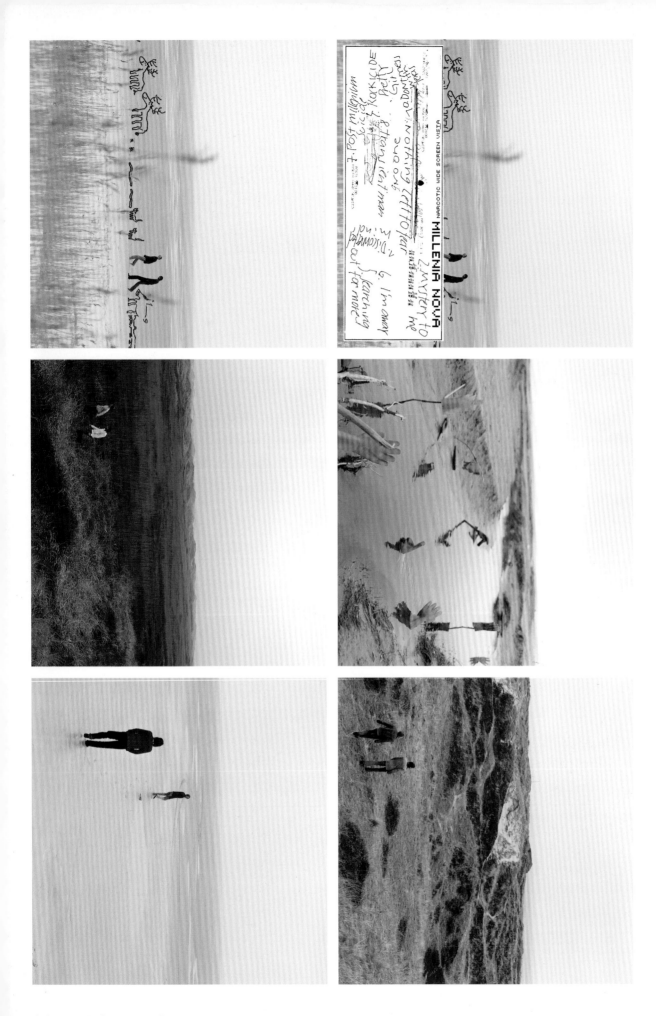

Slut

Nothing Will Go Wrong • Falling Down • I Can Wait
Time Is Not A Remedy • Easy To Love • Reminder
Universal • Something To Die For • Blow Up
One More Day • No Flowers, Please

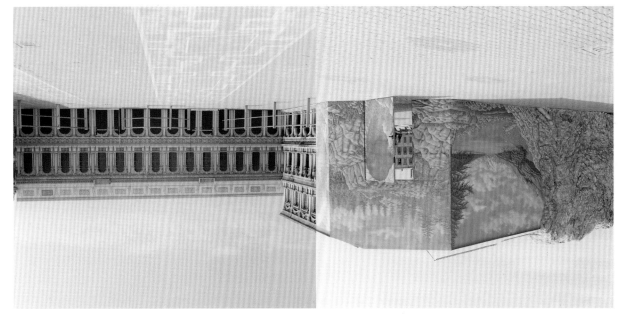

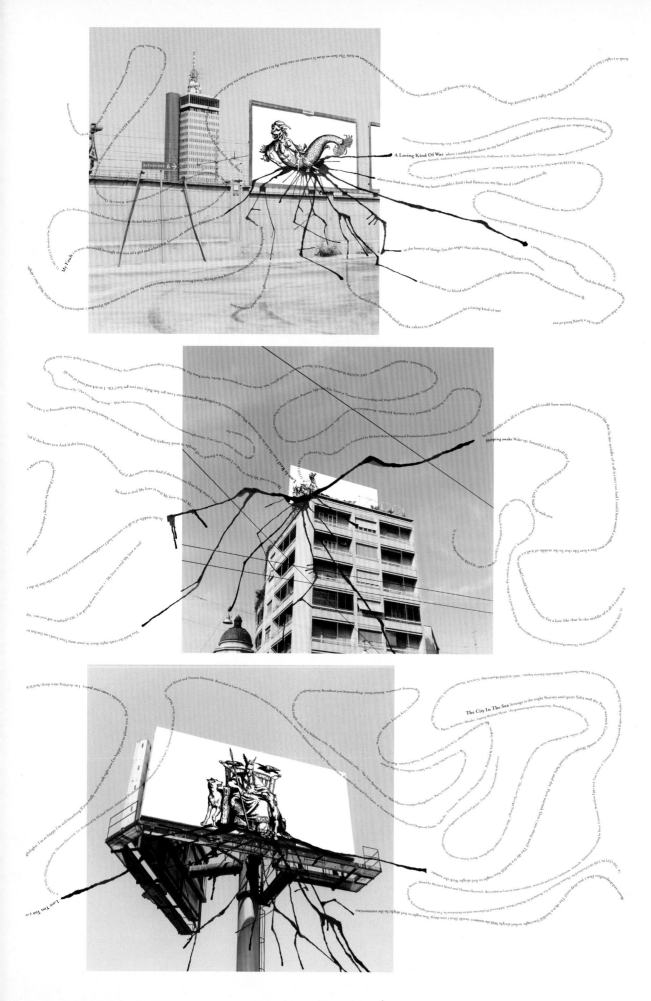

thom.

~ahead of the wav

1

2

**blackmail
friend or
foe?**

Dirk Rudolph

THE CHAP
THE HORSE
LCD36 LP36
Album out now
www.lorecordings.com
www.thechap.org

RE-CHARGING THE BATTERY

From his early Art Blakey-like drum assaults on 1960s South London through tonal explorations of percussion with today's laptop generation, AMM's Eddie Prevost has ceaselessly interrogated the meaning of sound and value of improvisation in a culture hostile to spontaneity, while keeping lines of communication open through his Matchless label and the Copula imprint he set up to publish his book No Sound Is Innocent. Words: Julian Cowley. Photography: Mattias Ek.

THE WIRE 37

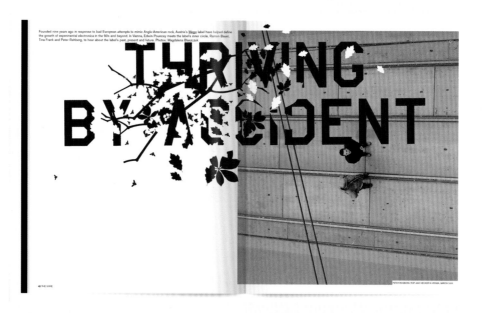

Founded nine years ago in response to bad European attempts to mimic Anglo-American rock, Austria's Mego label have helped define the growth of experimental electronica in the 90s and beyond. In Vienna, Edwin Pouncey meets the label's inner circle, Ramon Bauer, Tina Frank and Peter Rehberg, to hear about the label's past, present and future. Photos: Magdalena Blaszczuk.

42 THE WIRE

THRIVING BY ACCIDENT

PETER REHBERG (TOP) AND HELMUT IN VIENNA, MARCH 2003

1

2

Liselotte Watkins

～ Liselotte Watkins

Genevieve Gauckler

~ Rilla Alexander

Adam Pointer ⌒

1. Rilla Alexander - 2. Vår - 3. Paul Morrison

Rilla Alexander

⌒ Deanne Cheuk

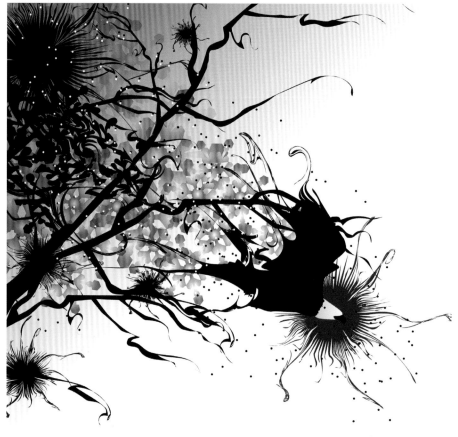

Toshifumi Tanabu

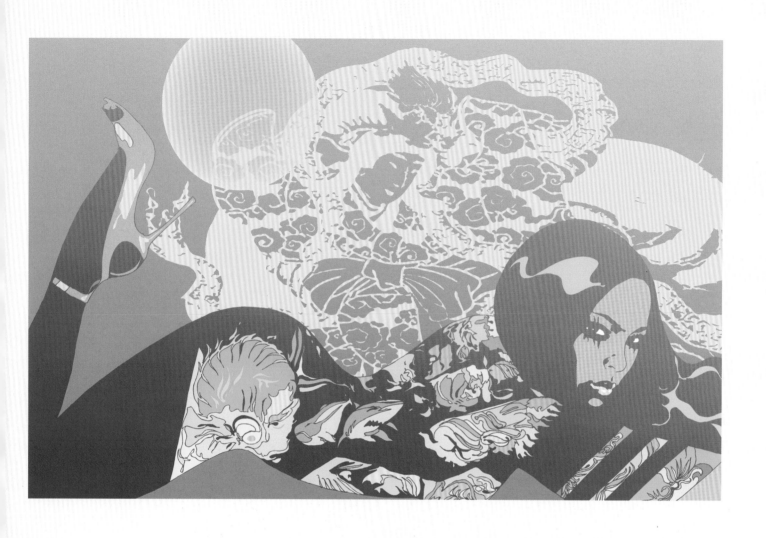

~ Kristian Russell

Joel Lardner

Joel Gardner ❧   ❧ 60

Fonho

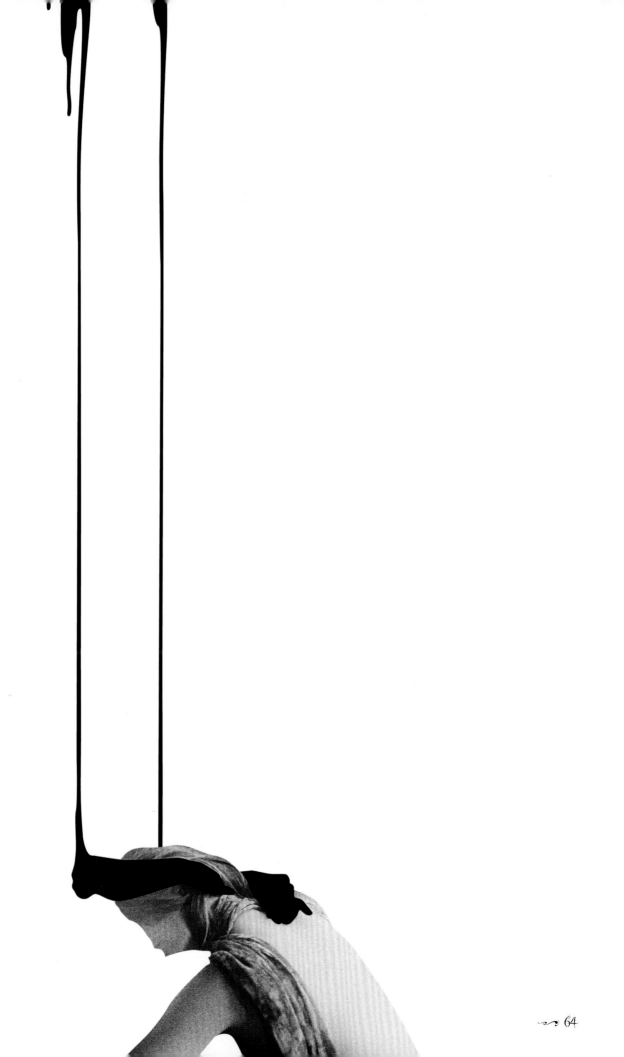

✑ Tonho

Justin Winz

Justin Winz

Justin Winz

Justin Winz

~ Roberta Nitsos

~ Peter Jeroense

Natsuki Lee

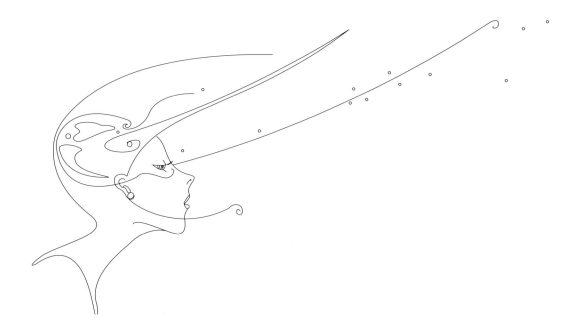

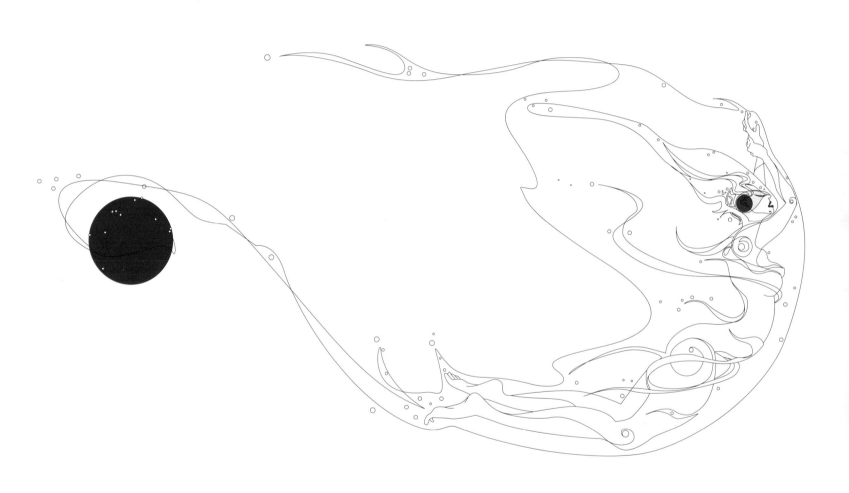

Natsuki Lee

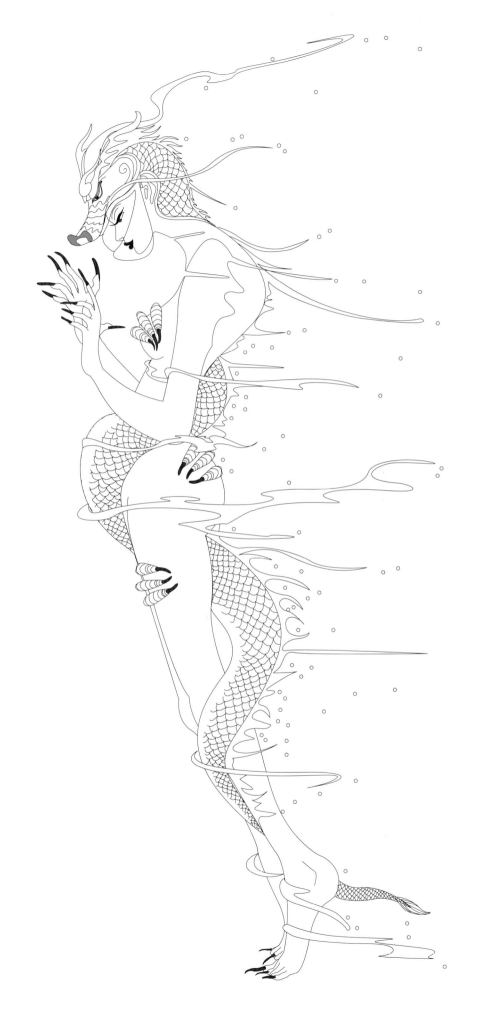

Natsuki Lee

find
love
once

_all

❧ Dirk Rudolph

1

2

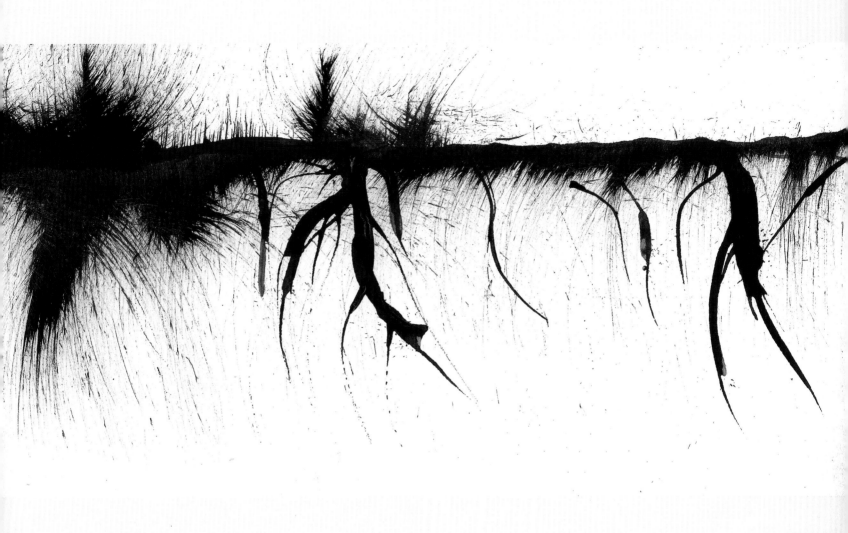

~ Dirk Rudolph

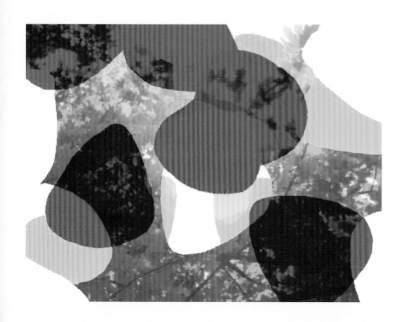

∿ Darren Watkins

❦ Guillaume Wolf

1

2

❧ 1. Jean-Jacques Tachiian - 2. Carine Abraham

BARASJÓNÞING 2003

SÝNINGASTAÐIR: GRANDROKK·DILLONBAR·KRÁIN · OPNUN 29.ÁGÚST

HRINGLEIKAR Í OLÍUDROPUM · ÞAÐ KU VERA HALTUR HUNDUR Í ÖLFUSI

GUÐMUNDUR ODDUR MAGNÚSSON GRAFÍSKUR HÖNNUÐUR

Toshifumi Tanabu

Xavier Cariou & Damien Beneteau

Dominik Gigler

1

2

1. Dominik Gigler - 2. Werner Amann

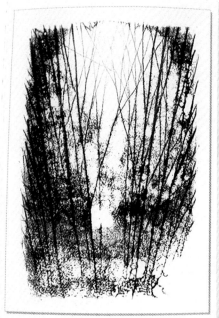

1

2

3

❧ Laura Movsavi

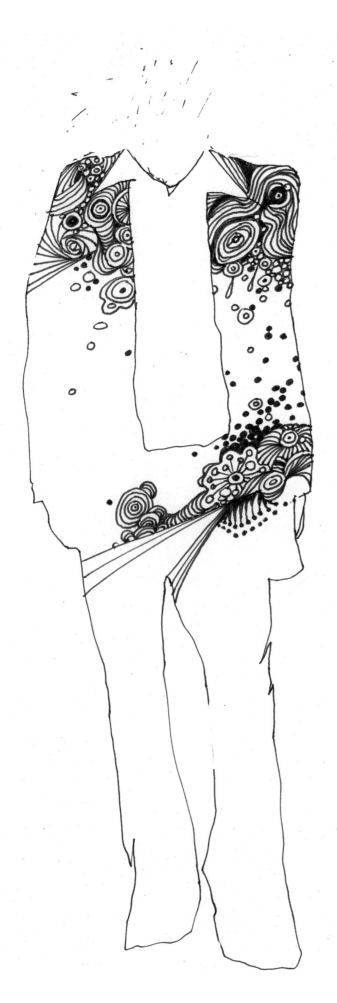

Seb Jarnot

~ Jane Bark

30 Jahre Jugend forscht 4000

ULTRASCHALL

November 200

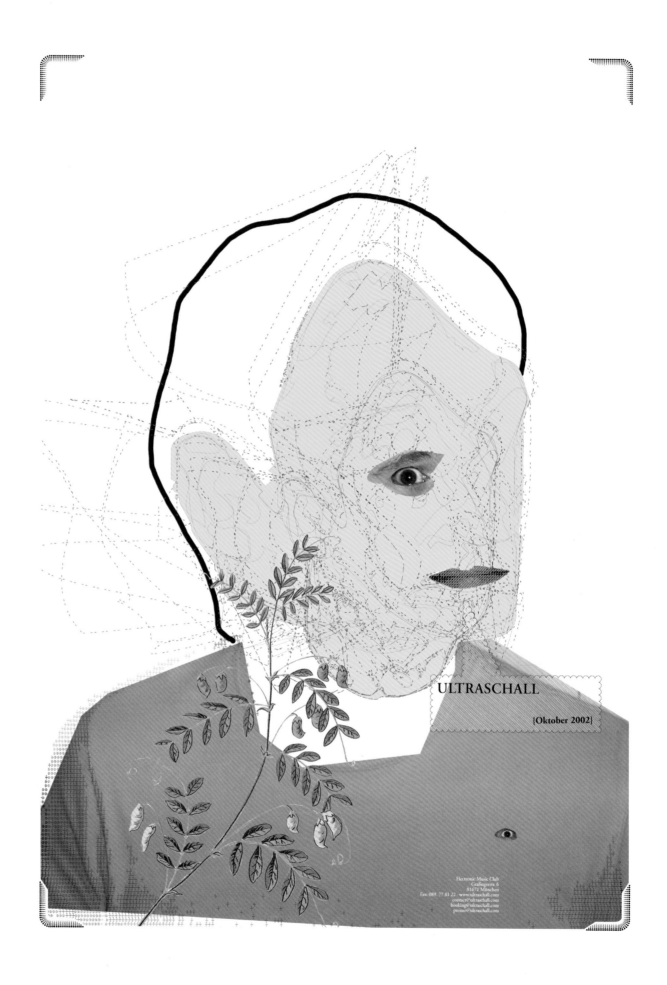

ULTRASCHALL

{Oktober 2002}

Electronic Music Club
Grafingerstr. 6
81671 München
Fax 089. 77 83 22 www.ultraschall.com
contact@ultraschall.com
booking@ultraschall.com
promo@ultraschall.com

Anne-Sophie Defoort

Jeff Soto

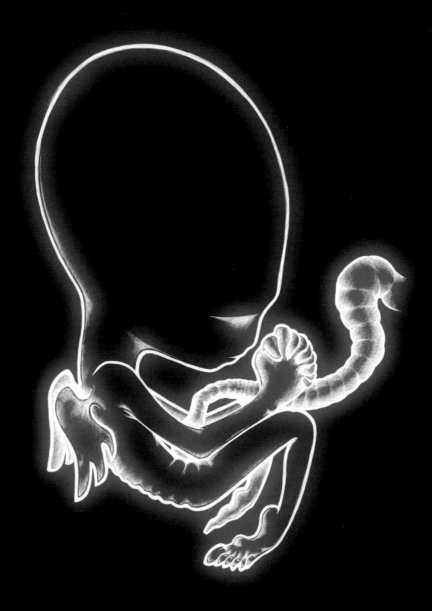

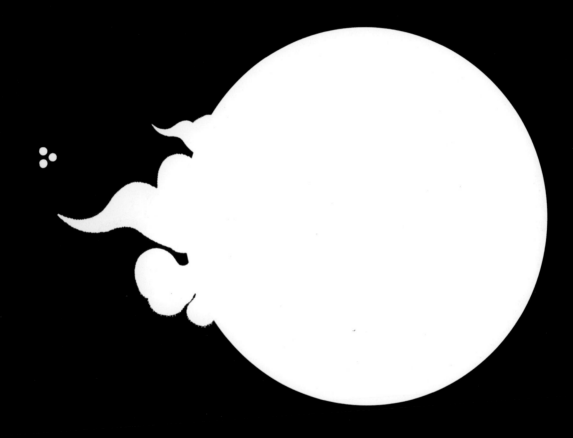

Index

Index